THE FIRST WAVE

CANCER SURVIVOR

CANCER SURVIVOR

THE FIRST WAVE

MARCOS COSTA

Story Terrace

I hope this book helps Cancer survivors, their parents, and friends to understand what the person who has Cancer need to build a better life.

HOPE.....FAITH.....LOVE

This book dedicate first to the God and for my mother, dad (Maria do Socorro and Eden Vieira), my brothers and sister (Flavio, Emerson and Ana Caroline), my aunt (Maria Jose), all family and friends.

CONTENTS

WEATHERING THE STORMS

Riding the waves of life is like entering the ocean to catch your first wave. You think you understand nature as you paddle your board, focused on your goal of surfing for a few brief moments. Gliding over the wave, everything feels perfect. But the ocean is unpredictable - waves come and knock you down, sucking away all your energy. You fight against the adversity until you are able to drag yourself back on board and continue paddling. Just when you least expect it, another massive wave crashes down on your head. And then another. That's life. Sometimes you think you're prepared, but life can change in an instant, like the force of waves in the ocean. It will knock you down, hurt you, and mess with your feelings. But you can't give up. With faith in God, you must find the strength to get back up and keep fighting. Battle through the pain and challenges to achieve your goals. Let difficulties make you stronger, wiser, better. Emerge reborn, ready to catch the next wave. Never surrender to the storms of life.

My life has been defined by this struggle against towering waves - unexpected health crises that attacked without warning. I was just a young boy in Brazil when the first massive wave hit...

Wave - Mother nature

MY EARLY CHILDHOOD IN BRASILIA, BRAZIL

I was born in 1968 in Brasilia, the capital city of Brazil, as the first child to my parents Eden and Maria. My father Eden worked as a representative for Philips lighting in our city, while my mother Maria cared for me and my younger siblings at home. We lived in a cozy house on a quiet street in a modest neighborhood of Brasilia. Our street had about 10 houses on each side, with kind Brazilian families and their children living in each one. Even though the houses were separate, we felt like one big neighborhood family.

My parents always said I was meant to be born in Brasilia, but my entrance into the world was not easy. When I was delivered, the umbilical cord had wrapped tightly around my neck, leaving me purple and barely able to breathe. The doctor swiftly removed the cord and I recovered, but it was the first of many health complications I would face in my young life.

Despite this rocky start, I grew into an active, energetic, blond-haired child with an outgoing personality. My endless curiosity got me into my share of mischief, like any young boy. But most of all, I loved playing soccer for hours on end with the other children on our street. We would gather all the kids together and play lively games of one-on-one, trying to kick the ball past each other in our makeshift goals of two piles of shoes. I remember racing up and down the street barefoot, the hot pavement burning my feet. But I didn't care - I just wanted to score another goal against my friends!

When I wasn't playing soccer outside, I enjoyed exploring the nearby woods and rivers with my friends, getting into all sorts of adventures. We were always scraping our knees and getting dirty, but it didn't faze us one bit. Our parents would shake their heads and yell at us to be careful whenever we came home filthy at dinner time. But they knew there was no stopping our energetic spirits and wild imaginations. We were just being normal, rambunctious boys.

By the time I was nine years old, our family had grown to include my two younger brothers Erasmo and Emerson, and a baby sister named Ana. Even though I was the oldest, I never treated my siblings as anything less than equals. We were partners in mischief and I loved making them laugh with silly jokes. Our parents Eden and Maria raised us to be respectful, compassionate children through their own quiet example. Family was everything to them, and they did their best to provide us a peaceful, loving home.

My mother's parents also lived nearby and were a huge part of my early childhood. My grandmother Corina especially doted on us grandkids. She knew all sorts of traditional folk remedies and would pick strange herbs from the forest whenever we had so much as a tummy ache. My skeptical father hated these "old wives' tales" but they seemed to work surprisingly well! Grandma Corina's homemade teas could cure just about anything as far as I was concerned. She was always there when I needed comfort or advice. I felt lucky to have such a caring extended family so close by.

In many ways, my early childhood in Brasilia was idyllic. I had loving parents, three best friends for siblings, a gaggle of neighborhood kids to play with, and a large, supportive extended family. But this childhood innocence was shattered when I was eight years old and had my first encounter with a life-threatening disease.

The day my childhood innocence was shattered started out like any other. I was nine years old, playing soccer in the street with my friends in our neighborhood in Brasilia, when a sharp pain suddenly shot through my right leg. I collapsed to the ground, screaming in agony. The excruciating pain in my femur was unlike anything I had experienced before. My frantic parents carried me home, giving me medication for the pain, but nothing helped. This was a deep bone pain that medicine couldn't touch.

After several days of unrelenting pain, my parents took me to the hospital. The doctors were perplexed, unsure of the cause. They put my leg in a cast from my chest down to my foot, hoping the immobility would help heal whatever was causing the pain. But the pain persisted. Exploratory surgery was scheduled to inspect my femur and see if they could determine the cause.

Little did we know, this was only the beginning of a long battle that would change my life forever...

Dad and Mon wedding

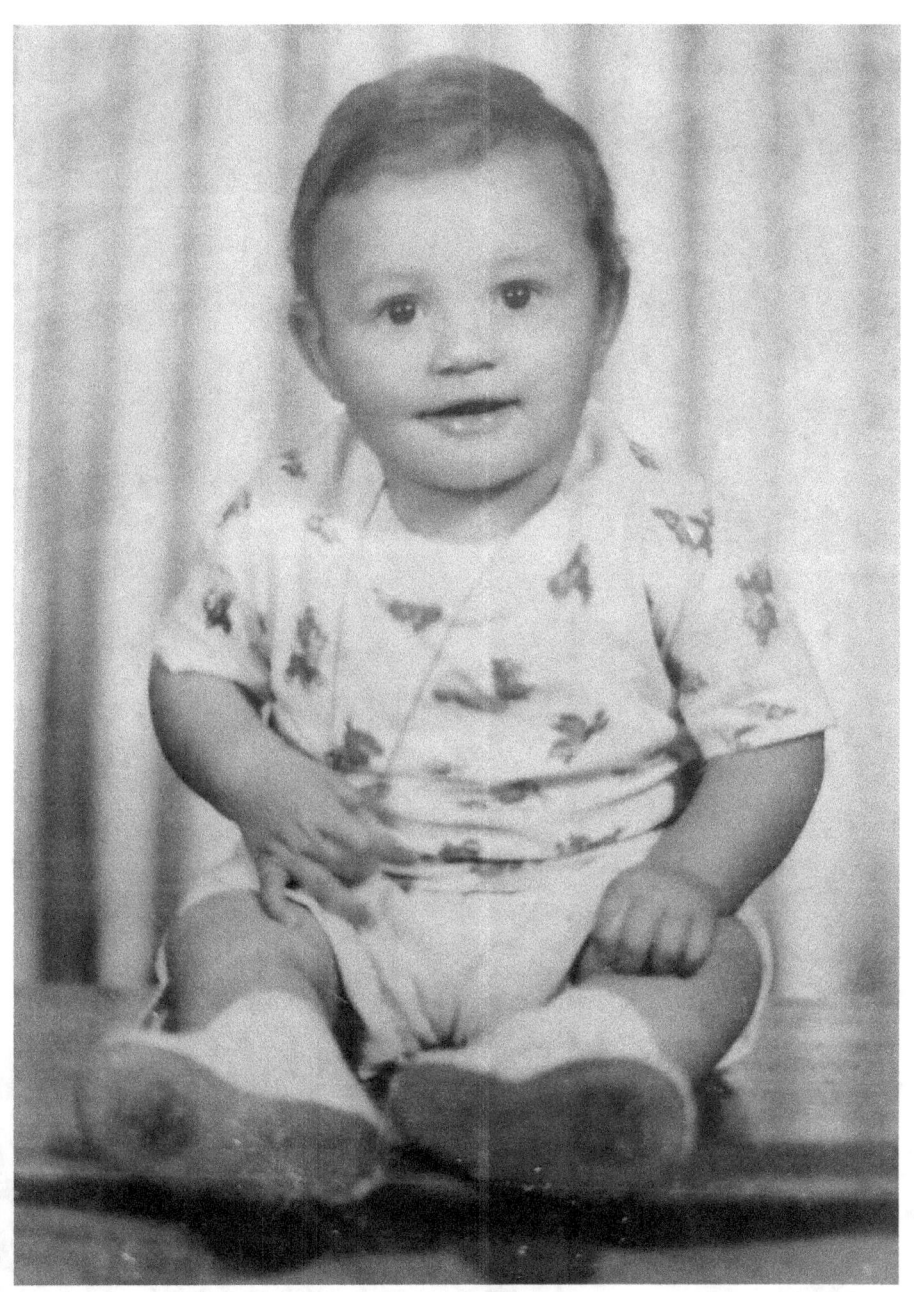

My little smile

1 years old

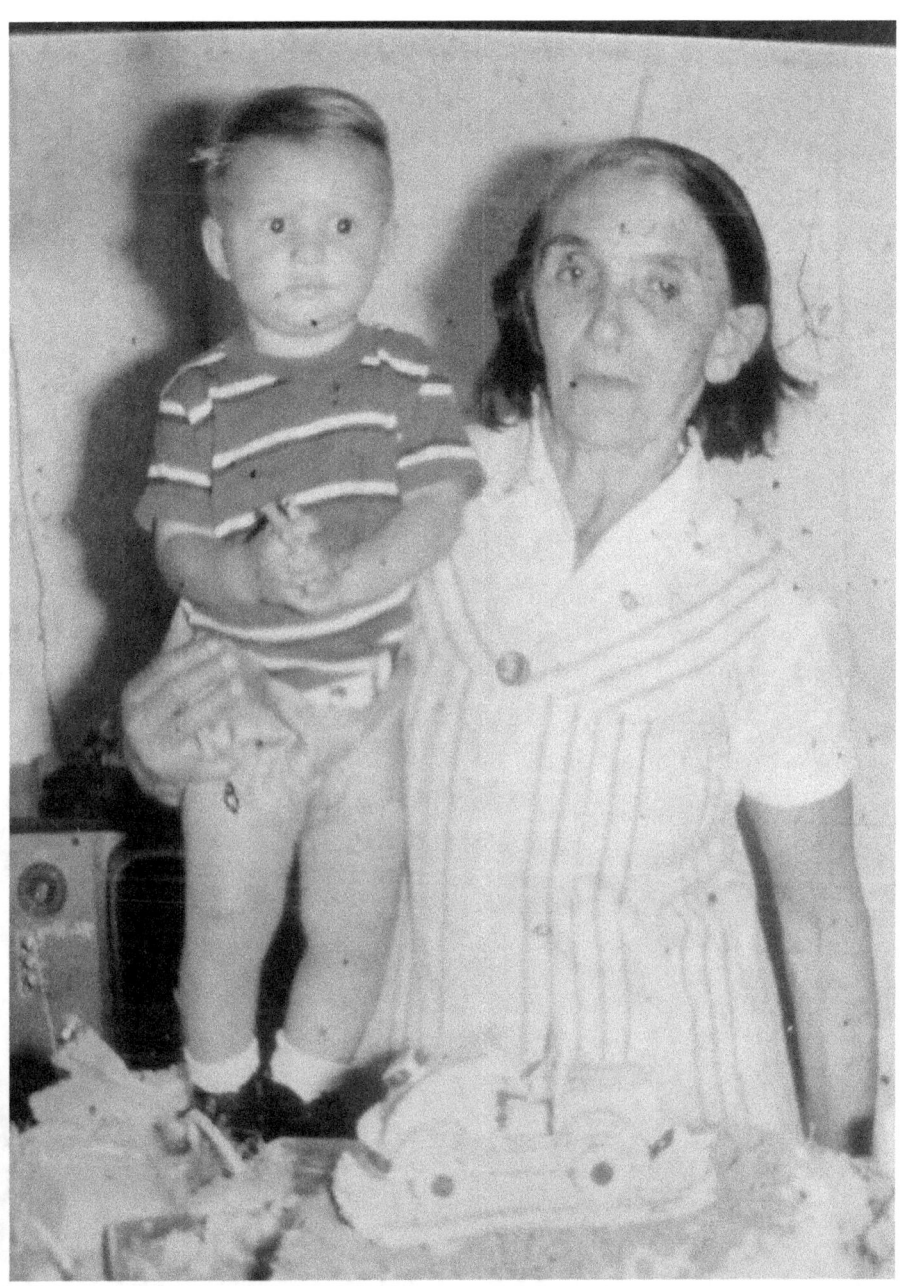

First birthday with my grandmother

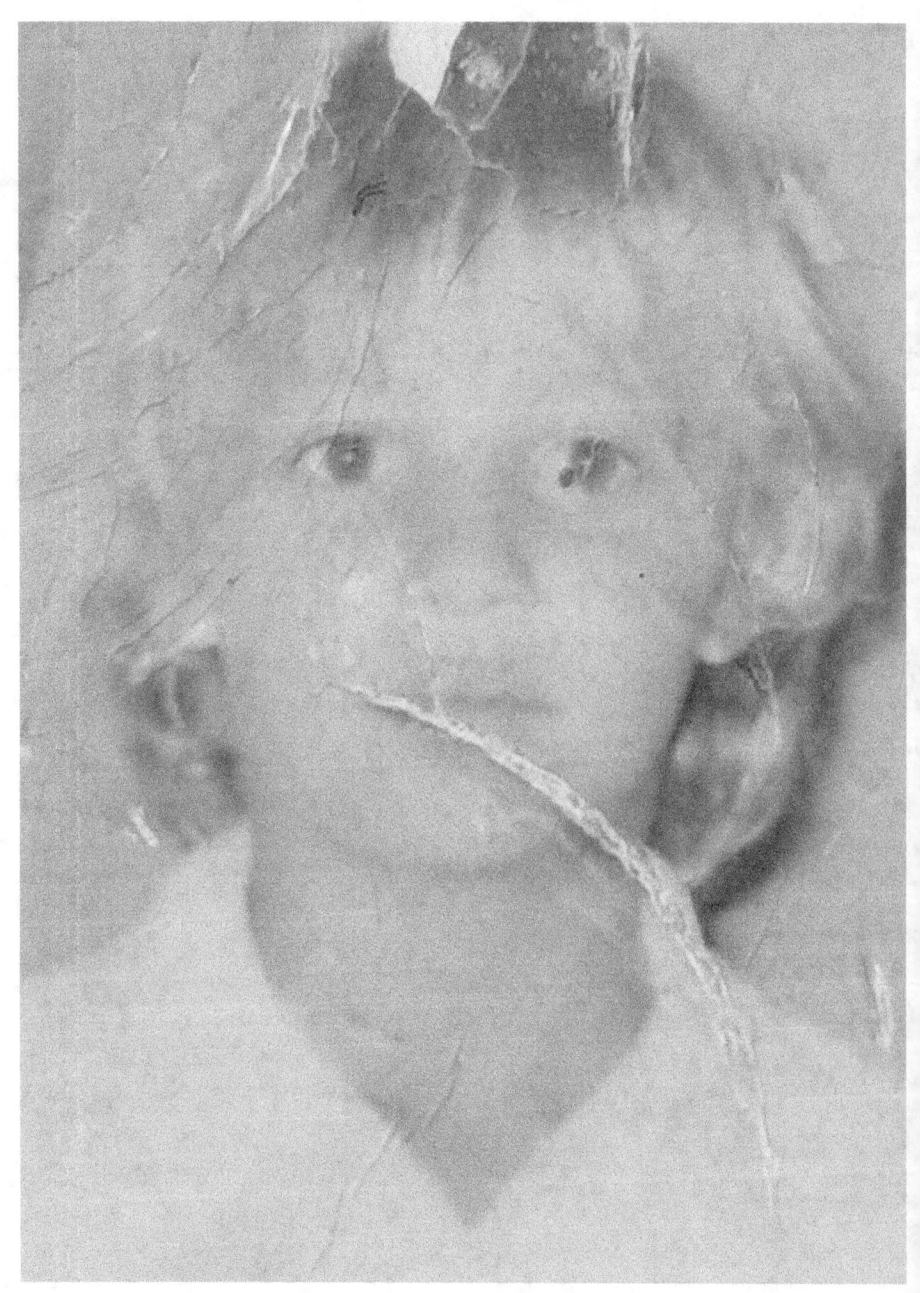

5 years old

MY FIRST BATTLE WITH CANCER AT AGE NINE

After several days of relentless pain, I was taken to the hospital for tests. The doctors discovered that the bones in my right femur were dangerously brittle, eaten away by what they suspected was a bone infection called osteomyelitis. I was immediately scheduled for surgery to remove the diseased section of bone. When I awoke, my right leg was encased in a heavy plaster cast from my chest all the way down to my toes. I would remain in this awkward full-body cast for over three months. My grandmother Corina helped to care for me since I could not even walk or go to the bathroom on my own.

One of our first priorities was to meet with an orthopedist to be evaluated and fitted for a leg brace. The clunky brace provided support from my upper thigh all the way down to my foot. It was custom made for my leg after multiple casts and measurements. Wearing it allowed me to walk and stand, but I could not bend my knee or ankle. For several months, I relied on crutches just to get around the house and manage basic mobility. My sweet grandmother moved in to help care for me while my parents worked. She patiently assisted me with using the bathroom, getting dressed, and maneuvering up and down stairs in our home. Her tranquil, nurturing presence and words of spiritual wisdom brought me comfort during this challenging transition period.

At the age of nine, seven months after starting to use the brace, I began taking short walks around our block with my grandmother's help. The physical therapist had me practice navigating stairs and regaining strength and balance in my withered right leg. The brace gave me a bit more mobility, but it was incredibly heavy and cumbersome to wear. I vividly recall struggling just to lift my leg while wearing that bulky metal brace. Yet day after day, I persevered with the mobility exercises, all the the goal of rebuilding muscle and one day walking independently again.

When the surgeons opened up my leg, they had discovered a large blackened area on my bone. The diseased section of bone was removed and biopsied. To my family's horror, the results showed I had a rare and aggressive form of bone cancer called Ewing's sarcoma. My shocked parents were told bluntly by the surgeon that there was no cure. I likely only had 3-6 months left to live. They should "give the boy anything he wants" and prepare for him to die soon.

My stoic father Eden was visibly shaken by my diagnosis. He avoided hospitals and didn't like seeing his son in so much pain. But my mother Maria and my aunt Maria Jose refused to accept the situation. They began researching my puzzling symptoms until they discovered Brazil's leading cancer treatment center in Rio de Janeiro. Though it pained her to be away from my brothers Erasmo and Emerson, my mother accompanied me and aunt Maria Jose to Rio in hopes of finding better medical care.

My parents were devastated, but my father's sister Maria refused to accept this death sentence. She traveled from Rio de Janeiro to Brasilia and insisted I be brought to Rio for further treatment. The best cancer clinic in the country was there, and she was determined to find me more options. My brave Aunt Maria became my fiercest advocate and second mother.

With the support of my aunt, my mother reluctantly left my father and younger siblings behind in Brasilia to accompany me to Rio de Janeiro. My father stayed behind to care for my two little brothers, while my mother and Aunt Maria escorted me to the cancer clinic in Rio de Janeiro. The community rallied around my father, bringing food and helping care for my brothers so he could manage without my mother. Their kindness meant everything during this difficult time.

In Rio, the doctors reaffirmed I had an extremely rare and aggressive bone cancer, but said they would do everything possible to save my life. They tested several different drugs on me, especially to boost my immune system. I started intensive chemotherapy treatments, receiving powerful drugs intravenously every week that made me violently ill. After one session, I vomited up so much blood that the doctors said I needed an immediate blood transfusion to survive. In their haste, they accidentally transfused me with contaminated blood that gave me hepatitis C, and I went into anaphylactic shock.

The excruciating chemotherapy drained the life out of me. For days after each weekly treatment, I was left completely bedridden and feeble.

Despite the tremendous physical and emotional toll, the aggressive treatments did slowly start to work. After over a year of weekly chemotherapy and radiation, the treatments were gradually scaled back to every two weeks, then once a month. I remained under close observation with regular follow-up visits. My aunt Maria kept a detailed diary of my treatments, medications and nutrition, wanting to fully document everything that was done to save me. Other doctors studied my case to advance cancer research, hoping my treatment protocols could help save others.

There were many times I felt ready to give up the fight, too weak and exhausted to go on. One day, as I lay in bed, I looked up and saw a photograph on the wall of the grandmother I had never met. I began speaking to her. "Take me with you," I said. "I can't fight anymore. I just can't go on." Hearing me talk this way to my departed grandmother brought my family members to tears.

I vividly remember one occasion where I was alone in my hospital bed, feeling sicker than I had ever felt before. An elderly woman suddenly appeared by my bedside, gently taking my hand in hers. She soothed me, saying "Don't worry, child. You won't die. Don't worry." This simple act of compassion resonated deeply, renewing my fading hopes. Though my family hadn't seen the woman, I know in my heart she was an angel sent to keep me fighting.

In addition to weekly chemo, targeted radiation therapy was administered directly to my right femur. My young body handled the toxic treatments poorly. I frequently felt like giving up, doubting I could be saved. Though still a child, the immense suffering I endured aged me beyond my years. I missed nearly two years of normal childhood experiences and activities. Whenever my family was able to visit Rio, it brought me immense joy. Their love gave me comfort during the darkest, most difficult chapter of my life.

The strong chemotherapy drugs also caused my long blonde hair to start falling out in clumps. My aunt took me to get my head shaved so I wouldn't have to watch my hair disappear strand by strand. She encouraged me to stay strong and keep up hope, even when I was at my sickest. Her faith in me gave me strength to keep fighting.

When I was diagnostic with cancer Ewing Sarcoma

Photo wit my Mon at school in Rio de Janeiro

With my dad, using my leg braces

MY TEENAGE YEARS REGAINING STRENGTH IN BRASILIA

B y the time I was fifteen years old, my doctors in Rio de Janeiro finally deemed me cancer-free. After nearly three grueling years of chemotherapy, radiation treatments, and multiple surgeries, I was ready to go home to Brasilia and start my life again as a "normal" teenager. My aunt Maria Jose, who had been my rock and fiercest advocate throughout my cancer journey, accompanied me on the flight back to my family. As the plane lifted off the runway, I remember feeling an overwhelming mix of emotions - relief, excitement, nervousness and uncertainty about what lay ahead.

My poor right leg, the focal point of my treatments, still felt quite weak and compromised after everything it had endured. Before sending me home, my oncologist advised me to "protect that leg" and avoid any strenuous physical activities that could cause further injury or strain. He knew my personality well, even as a young child, and warned that I should refrain from contact sports like soccer. I had always been an active kid playing sports with friends, so this was difficult advice for my rambunctious spirit to hear. However, I respected the doctor's orders, especially after all he and his team had done to save my life.

My energy level remained quite low that first year back, so I spent a lot of time resting in bed or on the living room sofa. But I was determined not to let cancer define my future.

Despite my physical limitations, I was eager to resume activities with friends and feel "normal" again. My parents worried about me reinjuring my leg. They also worried about my immune system, but they understood my burning desire to participate. Luckily, I discovered that volleyball was a sport I could play without much discomfort or risk. I joined my high school's recreational team and found that the lateral movements did not bother my leg compared to running sports. My friends were impressed that I could still spike the ball with power, despite lingering weakness on my right side. Playing volleyball made me feel like a regular teenager again. Our team played competitively against other local schools. Some schoolmates who knew my family pitied me, but I quickly proved them wrong on the volleyball court and earned admiration for my perseverance.

Interestingly, whenever I had to go to the hospital for any reason, I would always tell the doctors that I was a cancer survivor. I was such an active, healthy-looking boy, they didn't believe me.

Around age 17, I got involved in the martial arts of Judo, Taekwondo, and Kung Fu. I also took up surfing as a new hobby. From my first ride on a surfboard, I absolutely fell in love with it! Of course, I was cautious at first and stuck to smaller swells along the shoreline. My balance was not great starting out, and I took some hard spills getting knocked around by the waves. But I persisted and was determined to conquer those first tricky waves. For me, surfing symbolized the freedom, strength, and renewal I had worked so hard for after cancer's devastation. Each time I caught a great wave and smoothly rode it all the way to shore, I became more confident in my body's resilience. I spent countless hours practicing the technical skills of paddling, popping up on the board, and maneuvering. The mental focus required while surfing was actually therapeutic, helping me put cancer permanently behind me, where it belonged. My leg often ached after long surfing sessions due to lingering nerve damage. However, being in the ocean with my board felt so uplifting that I considered the mild pain a small price to pay for such exhilaration.

During my recovery at home in Brasilia, I also discovered creative interests like writing, music and dancing. Pursuing these passions filled a deep longing to reclaim the childhood years I had lost to hospitals, treatments and isolation. Writing poetry or song lyrics gave me a private outlet to process my cancer journey. The guitar became another close confidant, as I taught myself to play by ear and turn my words into songs. Though I lacked formal music training, I eventually joined a local band as their guitarist and back-up vocalist. Our band played small venues around town, mostly laid-back bars popular with university students. I had such fun bonding with my bandmates while developing raw talent into a budding musical gift.

Dancing evolved into a true delight that made me feel carefree and alive like never before. I enrolled in a variety of dance - samba, forro, zouk, jazz, contemporary - and found I had a natural aptitude for moving with rhythm. My personal dance style fused elements of traditional Brazilian folk genres with some modern flare. Dancing allowed me to fully release myself into the music, forgetting all limitations or struggles of the past. I practiced for hours in my bedroom mirror, admiring the growing strength of the leg that doctors once thought I might lose. Moving my body to those vibrant beats washed away residual traces of sickness, replacing them with pure joy. I felt such pride watching my teenage reflection dance with grace and poise.

Incredibly, I had continued attending my regular high school classes even throughout the worst of my cancer treatments. Of course, my aunt or parents drove me to and from school each day in Rio, since I was too weak for the bus. I often had to wear a protective face mask to shield my immune system during active chemo sessions. My teachers allowed flexible absences as needed for doctors' visits or if I was not well enough for school. While academic studies helped provide some sense of routine amid the chaos of cancer, I found socializing with classmates much more awkward and challenging. Seeing my peers carefreely enjoy their teen years accentuated all I had lost to relentless treatments and isolation. Though I graduated high school along with my age group, I did miss nearly two full years due to the demands of my medical care.

By my late teens, through determination and hard work, I had largely rebuilt the physical strength sapped by cancer and aggressive treatments. My leg would never be 100% normal, but through sports like volleyball and surfing, I proved my body's resilience time and again. I surrounded myself with positive friends who encouraged me to keep pursuing all that brought purpose and happiness. Staying active in the ocean and playing team sports made me feel "normal" once more. The creative arts allowed me to come into my own, discovering untapped talents to bolster a poise beyond my young years. I did not feel limited by my health challenges - if anything, they gave me a deeper appreciation for life's simple gifts.

While cancer permanently shaped me, it did not define my future. I was eager to follow my dreams and make the most of my second chance at life. As I looked ahead with optimism to all that lay in store as a young adult, I felt grateful for the remarkable woman I was becoming. My next chapter would unfold far from the watchful eyes of my aunt and mother. The time had come to take charge of my destiny and put into practice all the strength, courage, and wisdom instilled in me along my path to healing. I was ready to spread my wings beyond the familiar streets of Brasilia and embrace a world of possibilities.

Star playning guitar

Volleyball at school with my friends

BECOMING AN ADULT AND MOVING TO AMERICA

My first trip to America came unexpectedly in 1996 when I was 28 years old. I had been married for 7 years to my first wife, and we were living a comfortable life in Brasilia. I had a good government job and we owned a car - by Brazilian standards we were doing quite well. But my brother Erasmo had moved to the United States and he encouraged me to do the same. My first wife and I decided to take a leap of faith and move to Boston.

Leaving my tight-knit family behind in Brazil was difficult. I missed my parents, siblings, extended relatives and close neighborhood friends. But I was also excited for the adventure. When the airplane lifted off the ground, I took my first wife's hand and said, "Here we go, ready for our new life!" She squeezed my hand tightly and replied, "I'm ready."

Those first few years in America were filled with wonder and discovery. I was enthralled by the tall skyscrapers, massive highways, diverse neighborhoods and mouthwatering restaurants representing cuisines from around the world. On weekends we would pick a random destination and just start driving, exploring small towns and scenic landscapes from New Hampshire to Pennsylvania.

Back in Brazil I had dreamed of visiting Disney World, so when I stepped foot onto Main Street USA, I felt like a child again. We must have ridden Space Mountain ten times! And I'll never forget seeing my first baseball game at Fenway Park. The fans were so passionate, cheering for the Red Sox as we ate hot dogs and took pictures with the Green Monster.

While I was falling in love with America, it was also painfully difficult being so far from my family. We were used to Sunday dinners with 20 relatives crowded around the table, loud conversations and laughter echoing off the walls. Now it was just the two of us eating takeout and watching American television we could barely understand.

I tried to call my parents every Sunday but still missed seeing their faces and being able to hug them. When my aunt Maria Jose became ill, I flew back right away to be by her side at the hospital. Though she was unable to speak, the way her eyes lit up when I entered the room spoke louder than words. I held her hand as she took her last earthly breaths. My heart ached as I attended her funeral and said good-bye.

Jacqueline and I moved back to Brazil, but after eight month of living there, we made the difficult decision to divorce. Though the marriage ended, we parted on good terms after many happy early years together. I was glad to have experienced America but also relieved to be back home.

Returning to Brazil felt like slipping on my favorite old sweater - warm, comfortable and familiar. I reconnected with childhood friends who were amazed to see me, calling me "The Highlander" since I had improbably survived a grim cancer diagnosis as a child. I fell back into my old routine, working again for the Brazilian government and spending weekends barbecuing with my parents and siblings.

My social life also picked up. One night I was out dancing with friends at a lively bar in Brasilia. I noticed an attractive woman who had boldly taken a chair from my table. On purpose, I bumped into her from behind. When she turned around, I apologized for the intrusion and we began talking. Her name was Simone and she caught my eye because she was more reserved than the usual loud, boisterous girls. I asked her for her number and was delighted when she agreed to go on a date.

Always a romantic, I sent Simone flowers at her office to get her attention the week after we met. My gesture worked because she was impressed. Our first date led to more dates and soon we were a couple. Things just felt easy and right with Simone. After two years of courtship, we got married in 2009 when I was 41 years old.

Unfortunately Simone was never able to get pregnant. Years ago, doctors informed me that the radiation treatments I endured as a child left me unable to father children. This was disappointing, but together Simone and I have focused on the bright side. We've enjoyed the freedom to be spontaneous and travel. My nieces and nephews have also brought much joy into our lives.

A few years into our marriage, we started to get the itch for another international adventure. Simone's dream was to become fluent in English, so we discussed moving to an English-speaking country. She had previously studied abroad in South Africa for a short time and had progressed so much. The idea of living in America came up since I was familiar with it.

In 2017, we took the plunge and relocated to Utah. My cousin lived in the Salt Lake City area and thought it would be a good fit for us. The plan was for Simone to enroll in an intensive English program while I tried to start a tech business with my cousin. Utah seemed full of opportunity.

Returning to America after so many years away was quite an adjustment. The pace of life seemed faster and technology was radically different. I marveled at smartphones and ubiquitous WiFi. The endless strip malls and parking lots stretching to the horizon overwhelmed me. And I struggled to keep up with rapid-fire English from flustered customer service reps.

Of course I also missed the leisurely pace of life in Brazil and spending time with my extended family. Holidays and traditions didn't feel quite the same in America. Building close friendships all over again in a foreign culture proved challenging too. Most days it was just Simone and I in our apartment, trying to overcome feelings of isolation.

Starting the tech business with my cousin didn't work out, but I eventually got hired selling cars. The flexible hours allowed me to explore hobbies like wake surfing at local lakes. I was surprised to discover a huge wake surfing culture in Utah, very different from ocean surfing in Brazil. Some friendly folks even invited me out on their boat after I joined a Facebook group for Utah surfers. I'm still working to master the tricks again.

One afternoon just two months after moving to Utah, an episode of high blood pressure led me to visit the ER. To my shock, a CAT scan revealed two tumors in my brain - the cancer had returned once more. My emotions swung rapidly from denial, fear, sadness and anger. I asked the doctor "That's serious? !"

But echoes of my aunt Maria Jose's stern voice from childhood cancer treatments surfaced: "You must fight for your life!" Though risky, I decided to undergo surgery to remove the largest tumor. With my brave wife Simone by my side, I managed to beat the brain cancer once more. I have MRI monitoring every six months now. So far, the remaining tiny tumor seems to be sleeping and hasn't grown. What an unexpected rollercoaster shortly after arriving in America again!

Now in my mid-50s, I feel grateful to be thriving despite statistically grim odds. Writing this book has given me the chance to reflect back on all the unpredictable twists and turns. My hope is that by sharing my story, I can offer encouragement to others battling cancer or undergoing life's many storms. The fight is worth it to gain the coming bright sun on the horizon, even if the pounding first waves knock you down.

The next chapter of my life continues. I don't know what unexpected events lie ahead. But I've learned to embrace life's changes and keep moving forward, come what may. The innocent, carefree Brazilian boy I once was could never have imagined the adventures ahead...

My wife and I in USA

THE SURPRISE RETURN OF BRAIN CANCER

Just as I was settling into my new life in Utah, I was blindsided by another health crisis. Severe headaches in late 2017 led to the shocking discovery of a large brain tumor, only months after moving to America. Facing high-risk surgery so soon after relocating was extremely difficult. But thanks to my wife Simone's loving support and my unshakeable faith, I found the strength to push forward. Staying positive kept me from being overwhelmed by fear and despair.

It was a typical day in November when I began experiencing high blood pressure. I knew my body well, having dealt with health issues in the past. Something felt very wrong. I told my wife that we needed to go to the emergency room, as I suspected my blood pressure was dangerously elevated. At the ER, the doctor confirmed my suspicions—my blood pressure was through the roof. As a precaution, she ordered a CT scan of my brain. I was not expecting anything catastrophic, but the doctor soon returned with a grave look on her face. She somberly told me that I had a tumor in my brain larger than a golf ball.

My wife Simone was in shock, immediately understanding the word "tumor" despite her still-limited English skills. We had only been in America for two months at that point. I remained eerily calm—after surviving childhood cancer and living through risky treatments, a brain tumor seemed less intimidating. The doctor wanted to admit me to the hospital immediately for further testing. At 5 AM the next morning, an MRI revealed I actually had two tumors in my brain—one large mass and one smaller growth.

The neurosurgeon explained that removing the tumors would be extremely high-risk given their size and location. He said I could possibly be left paralyzed, severely impaired or even die during surgery. The options were to live with the tumors and face an uncertain prognosis, or have surgery knowing the risks. Without hesitation, I chose surgery. The doctor somberly advised me to contact my family and say my goodbyes, just in case.

Facing yet another cancer threat after recently moving halfway across the world was almost too much to comprehend. Thankfully, I had my incredible wife by my side through it all. Her quiet strength and steadfast devotion kept me grounded. My optimism and faith never faltered. I firmly believed God had a plan for me, and that he would see me through this trial.

After nearly six agonizing hours of waiting, the surgeon emerged from the operating room. Miraculously, he was able to remove the largest tumor completely without any complications or damage to surrounding brain tissue. My relief was indescribable. As I regained consciousness, I immediately started speaking English to assure those gathered at my bedside that my cognition was intact. My wife wept with joy at the sound of my voice.

Recovery was slow and difficult. Having a section of skull temporarily removed created persistent headaches until that bone was surgically replaced. Enduring repeated brain scans and procedures was physically and mentally taxing. But my innate positivity urged me forward. I focused on healing, one day at a time.

Simone has been my faithful partner for over fourteen wonderful years now. During difficult moments like my brain cancer diagnosis, her quiet strength and unconditional love carried me through. She has a calming influence that makes me feel grounded. We still enjoy going out dancing and trying new restaurants together. I feel so blessed to have found my soulmate.

Though each tumor was benign, their presence was still a frightening reminder of my earlier cancer battle. Thankfully, follow-up tests and scans detected no remaining cancer cells, except for the remaining small tumor in my brain, which needed only one session of radiotherapy to keep it under control. However, the ordeal reinforced the sobering fact that I will never be entirely free from the threat of cancer's return. But that reality only strengthens my resilience and appreciation for life.

I still require scheduled MRI scans annually to monitor for any new growths. And lingering side effects like memory lapses are constant reminders of what I've endured. But I do not dwell on the past or future uncertainties. I stay firmly rooted in the present, finding joy in everyday moments.

Playing guitar and dancing lift my mood and soothe my soul. The spiritual fulfillment of volunteering is incredibly rewarding. My never-ending gratitude for my second chance at life motivates me to give back in any way I can.

The love and support of my family was instrumental in getting me through my darkest days. My wife's unwavering devotion was a gift from God. During my weakest moments, my faith did not falter. I never questioned why this was happening to me again. I knew God would give me the strength to keep fighting if it was His will. And by His grace, I survived.

Though I pray I will remain cancer-free forever, only God knows what the future holds. No matter what waves crash over me, I will continue paddling forward with faith and fortitude. My story does not end here. I have more good to do in this world. I want to comfort those who suffer and kindle hope in desperate hearts. I aim to turn hardship into healing, and transform my trials into triumphs that uplift others. The next chapter of my life's mission is just beginning.

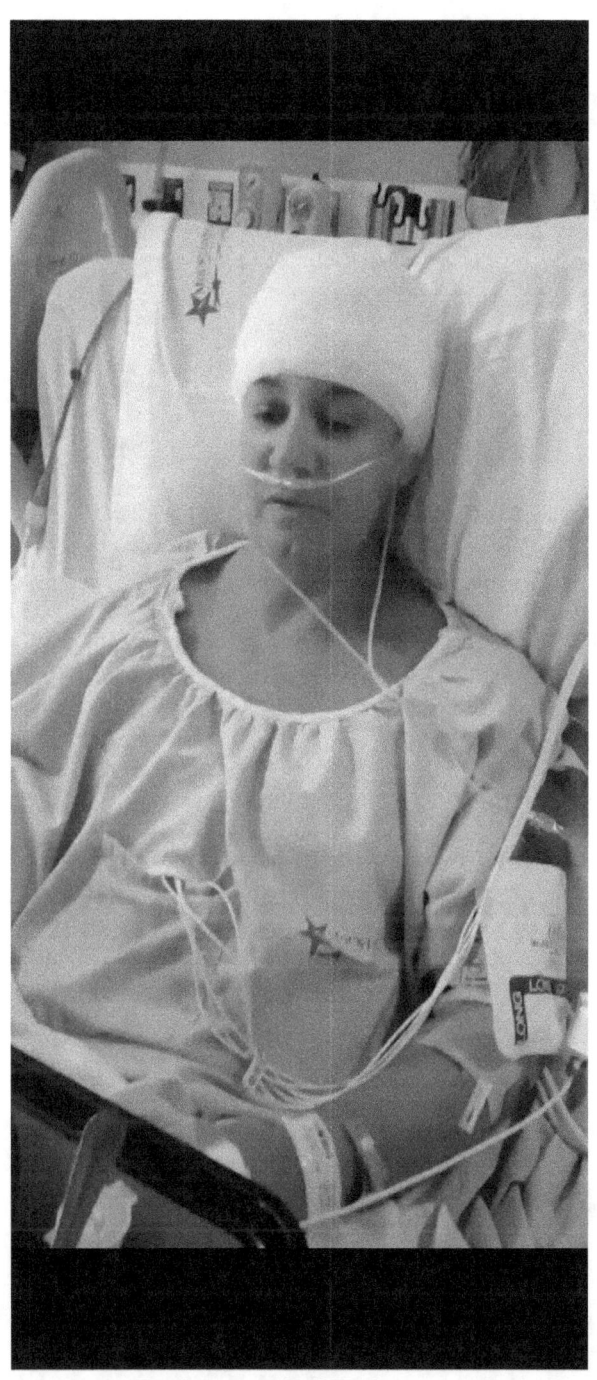

After brain surgery

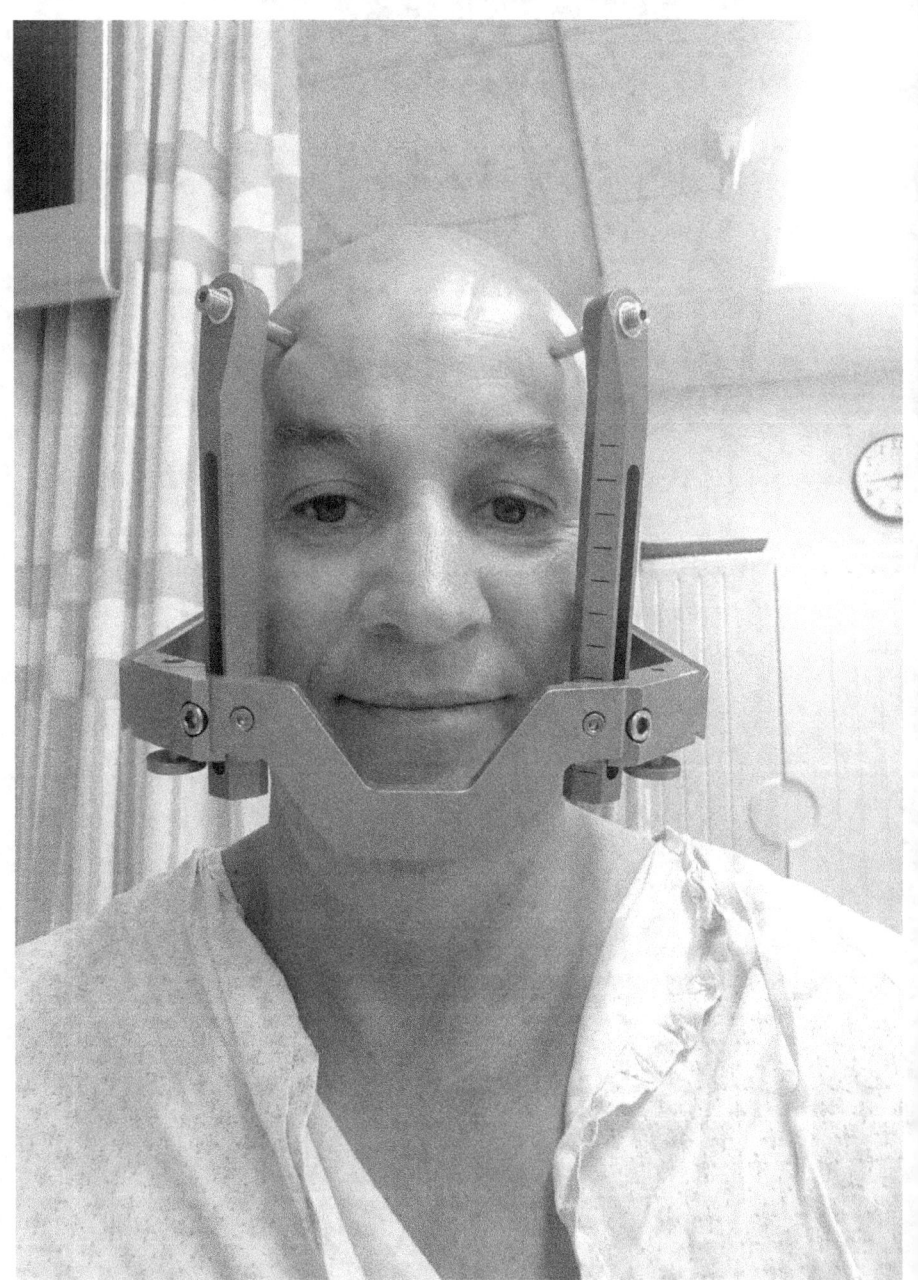

First radiotherapy in my brain - Always be positive

Recover from my brain surgery with my wife - Always smiling

TURNING THE TIDE

Facing cancer twice and overcoming the odds has given me a unique perspective on life. By sharing my story, I hope to provide comfort, wisdom and encouragement to others battling cancer. I want them to know that it's possible to still live life joyfully, even during the darkest times. My goal is to inspire people facing cancer to stay strong mentally and spiritually. My nonprofit organization will offer cancer patients and families spiritual and emotional support to complement medical treatment.

I have written this memoir to chronicle my life and cancer experiences. My intention is not to make money selling books, but rather to share my journey in hopes of helping others on their own cancer path. I want to empower people to realize that cancer does not have to define or limit them. As a lifelong surfer, I cannot help but compare the challenges I faced to the difficulties of riding a big first wave as a beginning surfer. The ocean can be unpredictable and that first wave is always the hardest to conquer. But with perseverance and the right support, one can get back up again after falling. Cancer too can seem overwhelming and unpredictable at first, knocking you down when you least expect it. But you can choose to keep fighting the waves, relying on your inner strength and faith to carry you.

I am in the process of launching a nonprofit organization to provide free services to cancer patients and their families. This will include counseling, support groups, retreats and financial assistance with treatment costs. Being able to give back and help others on their cancer journey is deeply rewarding for me. I know firsthand how invaluable support systems are when facing a devastating diagnosis. My own family gave me so much strength as a child battling cancer in Brazil in the late 1970s, when treatment options were limited. My mother and father never gave up hope, despite the doctor's grim prognosis that I only had months to live. My aunt became my second mother, fighting fiercely for me to get the best available treatment. She told me, "You have to fight. Fight for your life." Her faith in me gave me courage I needed to keep battling the cancer wave trying to pull me under.

Volunteer work is a blessing that allows me to give hope to others, just as my family gave me. I want to empower families of cancer patients to provide emotional and spiritual uplift to their loved ones. A cancer diagnosis affects the whole family, not just the individual patient. Parents of children with cancer especially need guidance on how best to support them while still allowing normal childhood experiences. Being overprotective or pitying can be harmful, while gentle encouragement fosters mental strength. My nonprofit will provide cancer families with counseling on navigating this difficult journey together in a constructive way. We will help relatives become a source of inspiration rather than unintended distress for their loved one facing cancer.

Having a purpose and passion outside of cancer is hugely important for staying motivated and joyful. This applies to both patients and their caregiver families. For me, music and dance have always been a creative outlet for self-expression. Playing guitar with my first band as a teenager gave me confidence and a positive identity beyond being "the kid with cancer." Later in life, I found a liberating new passion in wake surfing. The friends I made in Brazil's wake surfing community brought me back from the grief of divorce. After moving to Utah and enduring several brain tumor surgeries, I was able to wake surf again thanks to the loving support of fellow wake surfers I met locally. This reignited a sense of meaning and normalcy during my recovery. Through my nonprofit, I want to help cancer patients and families discover their own passions to provide an empowering focus beyond the cancer.

Volunteer activities can also be incredibly fulfilling by allowing one to contribute to others. While running a nonprofit organization in Brazil that assisted impoverished cancer patients, I found profound purpose in fundraising and raising awareness for this worthy cause. My current goal is to begin volunteering at local hospitals in Utah, as I did in Brazil. There is deep meaning in brightening someone else's day during their health struggles. I believe visiting and praying with patients fills not only their hearts, but your own. It helps us remember what matters most - human compassion.

Above all, my Christian faith has carried me through every challenge and given me strength to keep fighting. As a child with cancer, praying with my devout Catholic grandmother provided divine comfort amid fear and uncertainty. During those long days confined to my bed, unable to walk after surgery, grandma would reassure me of God's love and presence. She repeated the Bible verse, "Trust in the Lord with all your heart." Her steadfast faith became my own lifeline, keeping me anchored emotionally. My spirituality only grew stronger as cancer returned in my adulthood. Each time, I relied on my relationship with God to guide me into the light. Now I wish to share this gift with others who feel alone in the darkness of a cancer diagnosis. My nonprofit will provide spiritual counseling and prayer support according to each patient's beliefs, meeting them wherever they are spiritually.

Even after cancer returned to my brain in 2017, I chose to remain focused on living life to the fullest rather than being consumed by worry. Initially I feared my dream of starting a family would be shattered, given the aggressive treatments required. However, with prayer and faith, those fears faded. My wife's constant love and my trust in God's plan for my life have brought me peace. I know my purpose is to help others battling cancer remain hopeful no matter the prognosis.

My story proves you can still find joy and keep fighting no matter what waves cancer sends your way. Beginning surfers learn quickly that the ocean does not yield easily to our determination - mounting the board again and again after being tossed will only lead to exhaustion. However, by patiently waiting for the right moment, we can "let the wave take us," then gently rise up. Fighting cancer demands similar patience, intuition and harmony with forces beyond our control. Dark moments will come when you wipe out. But the light always returns to guide you home. Faith in this gives you power to keep paddling out, awaiting the next perfect wave with open arms.

In conclusion, I have endured the trials of cancer so that I may shed light for others still finding their way through the darkness. By sharing my story and offering spiritual support through my nonprofit organization, I hope to help cancer patients and families discover renewed purpose, passion and peace on their journey. Though the first waves are the most daunting, take heart - you have already proven your resilience by daring to paddle out at all. The path before you may be uncertain, but your courage will see you through to distant shores. With acceptance, active love and abiding faith, you too can learn to ride life's wildest waves.

Find myself, never give up

After years of battle - Never give up, fight for your life.

USA Wakesurf Competition - 2nd place - Be strong

Gratitude - God is everything

StoryTerrace